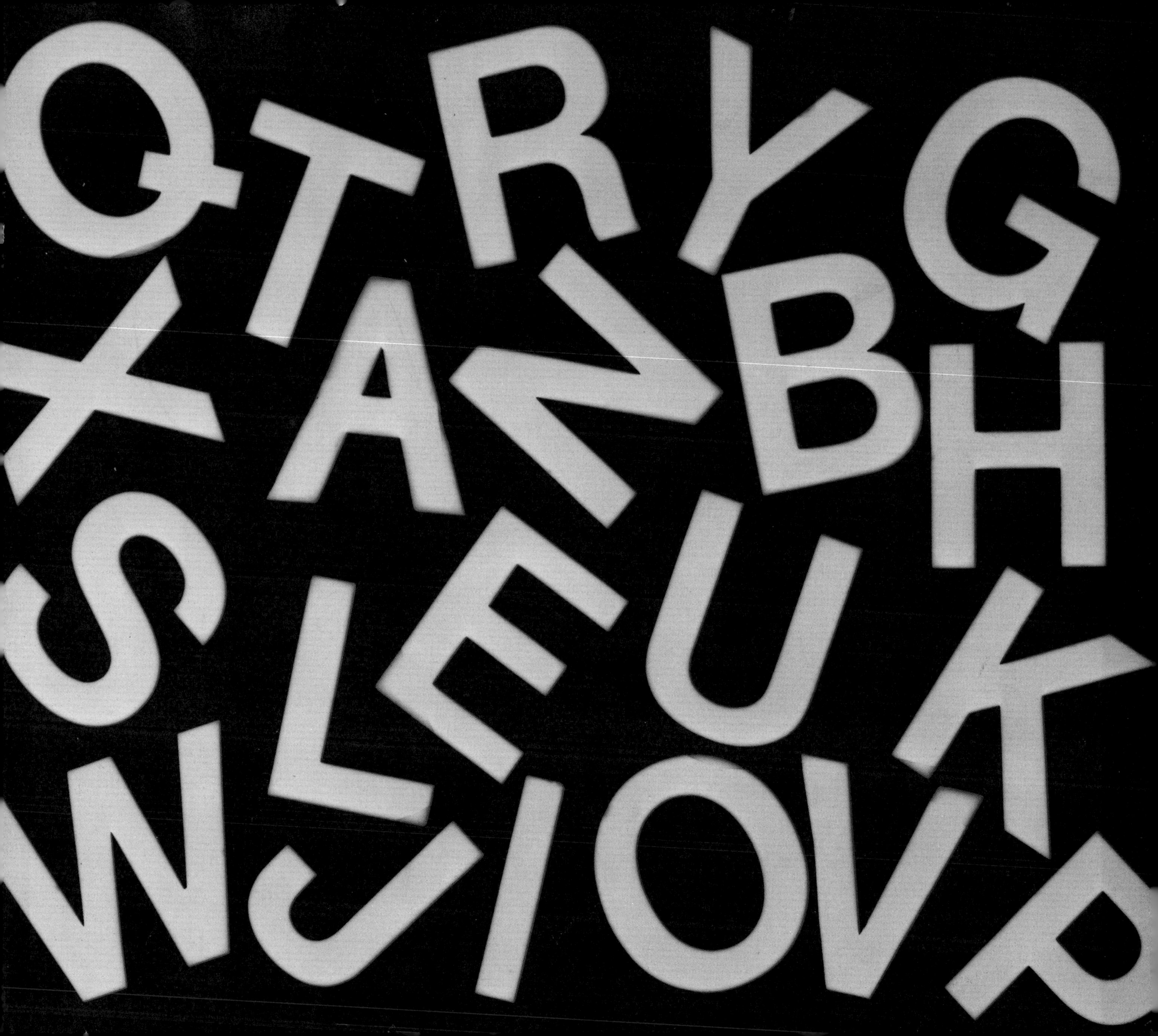

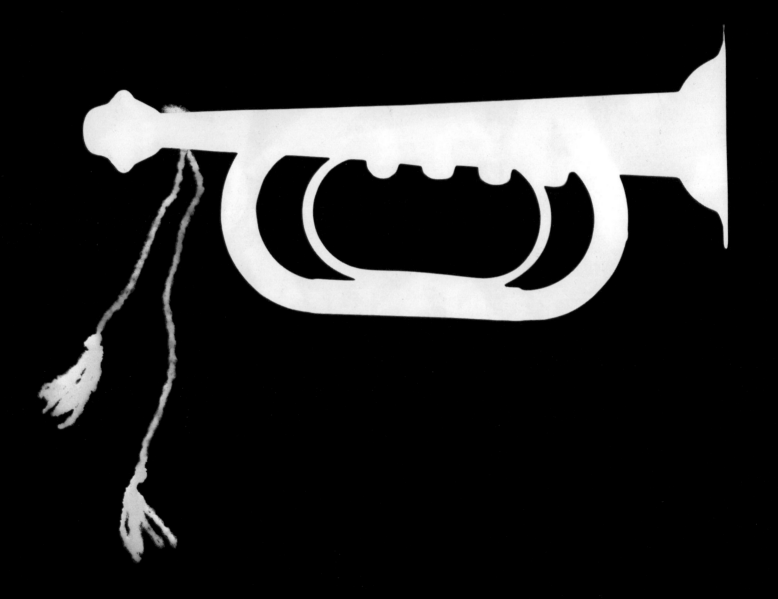

A, B, See!

by TANA HOBAN

Greenwillow Books, New York

Library of Congress
Cataloging in Publication Data
Hoban, Tana.
A, B, see!
Summary: A collection of photograms
of objects which begin with a
particular letter of the alphabet.
1. English language–Alphabet–Juvenile
literature. [1. Alphabet] I. Title.
PE1155.H58   [E]   81-6890
ISBN 0-688-00832-1   AACR2
ISBN 0-688-00833-X (lib. bdg.)

This one is
for Miela

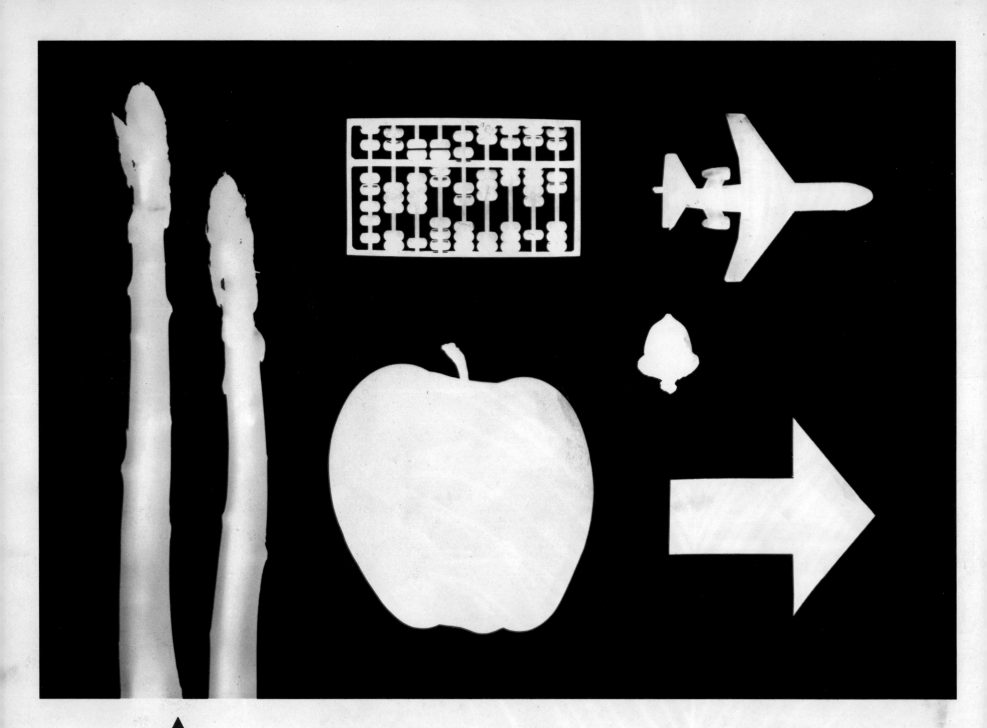

A BCDEFGHIJKLMNOPQRSTUVWXYZ

ABCDEFGHIJKLMNOPQRSTUVWXYZ

AB**C**DEFGHIJKLMNOPQRSTUVWXYZ

ABC**D**EFGHIJKLMNOPQRSTUVWXYZ

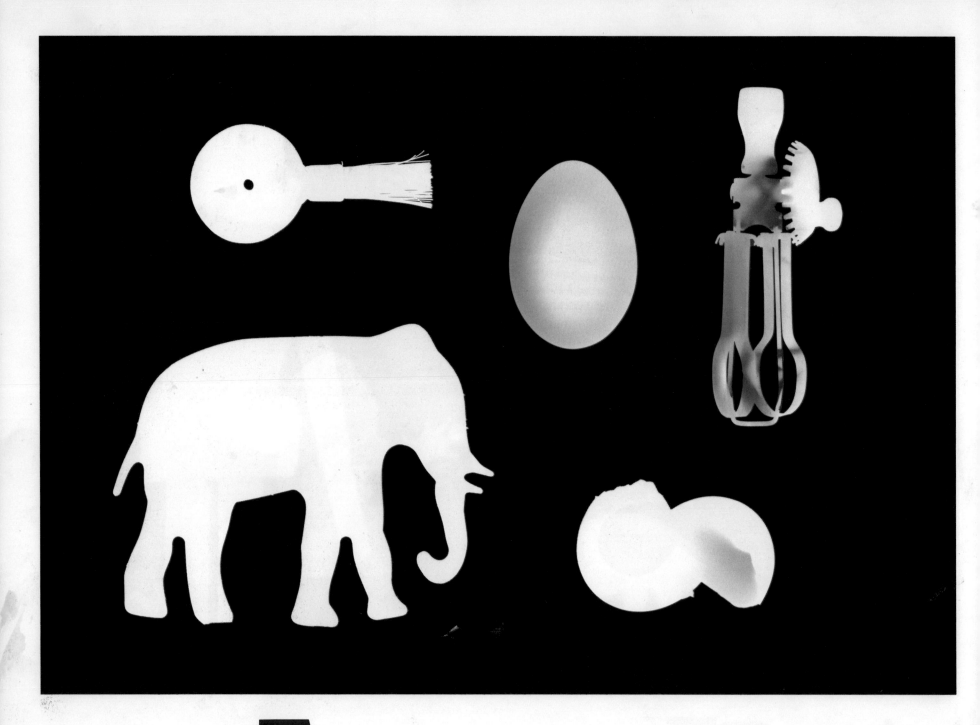

E

ABCD **E** FGHIJKLMNOPQRSTUVWXYZ

F

ABCDE **F** GHIJKLMNOPQRSTUVWXYZ

ABCDEF**G**HIJKLMNOPQRSTUVWXYZ

H

ABCDEFG**H**IJKLMNOPQRSTUVWXYZ

ABCDEFGH **I** JKLMNOPQRSTUVWXYZ

ABCDEFGHI**J**KLMNOPQRSTUVWXYZ

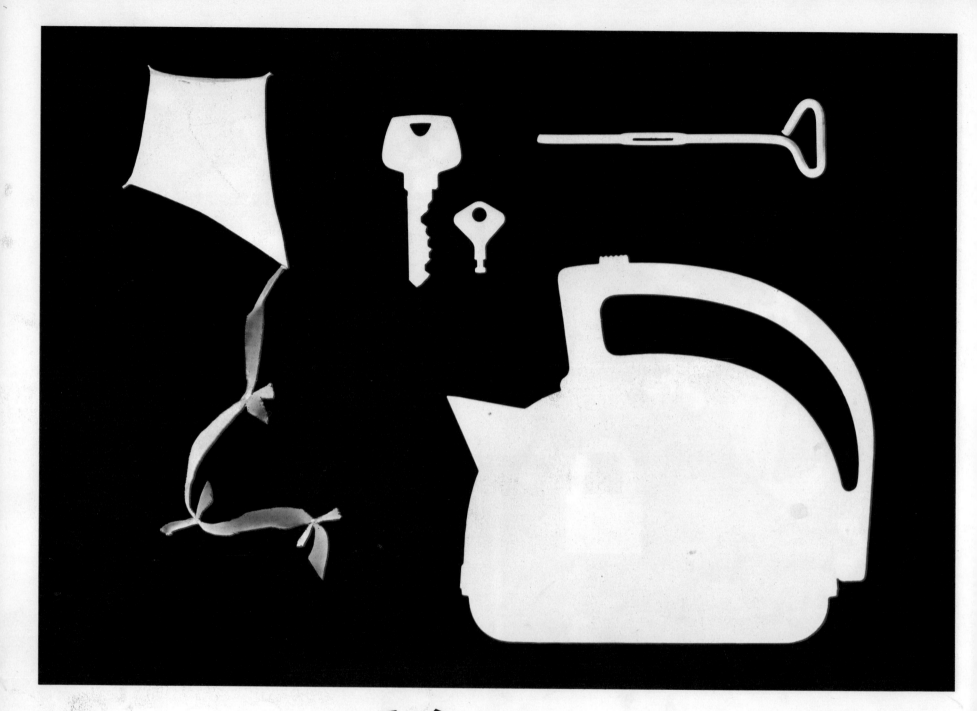

ABCDEFGHIJ**K**LMNOPQRSTUVWXYZ

L

ABCDEFGHIJK**L**MNOPQRSTUVWXYZ

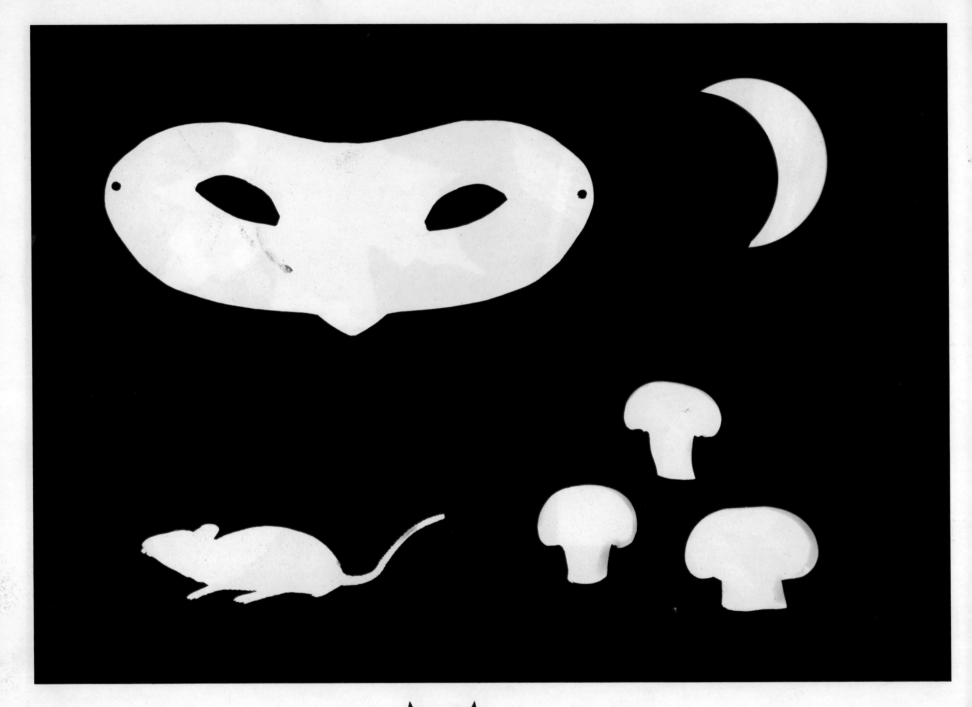

ABCDEFGHIJKL**M**NOPQRSTUVWXYZ

ABCDEFGHIJKLM**N**OPQRSTUVWXYZ

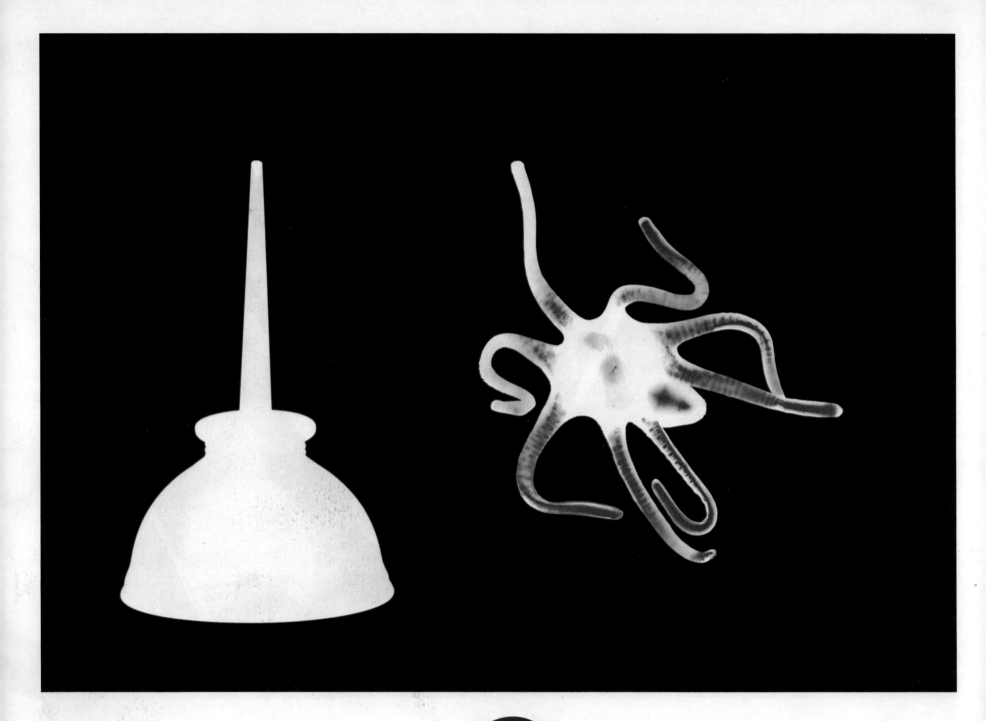

ABCDEFGHIJKLMN**O**PQRSTUVWXYZ

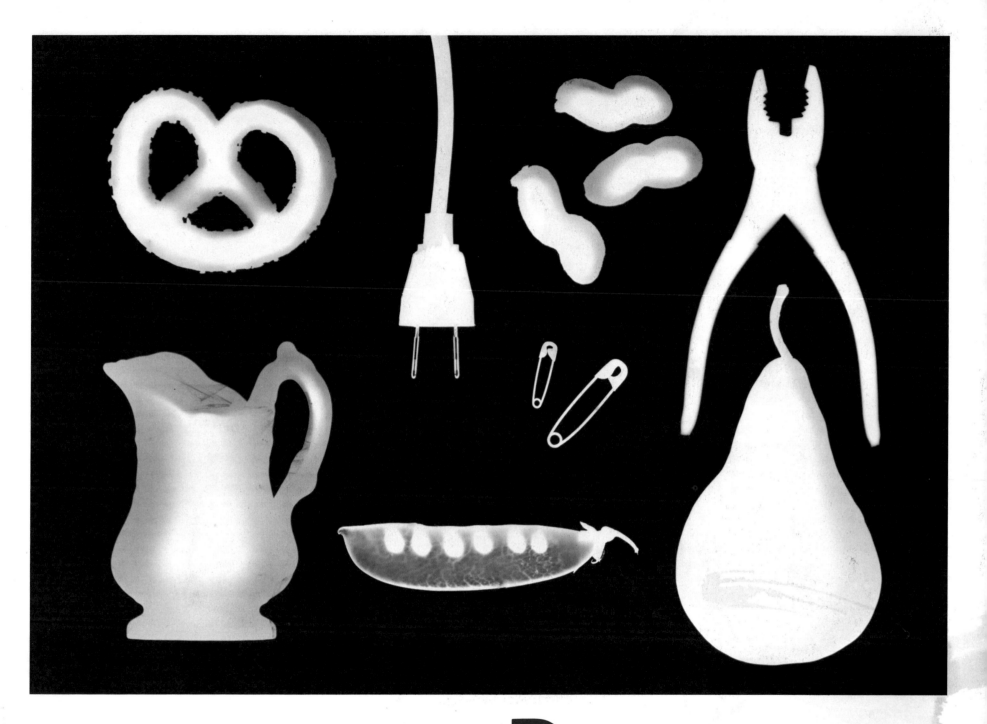

ABCDEFGHIJKLMNO**P**QRSTUVWXYZ

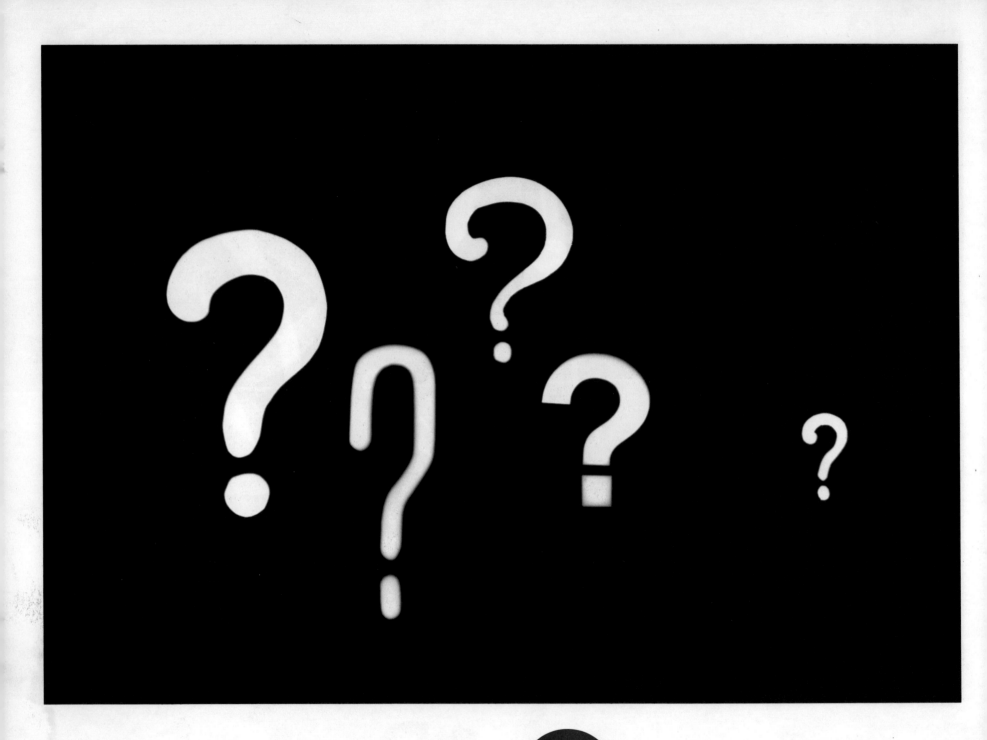

ABCDEFGHIJKLMNOP**Q**RSTUVWXYZ

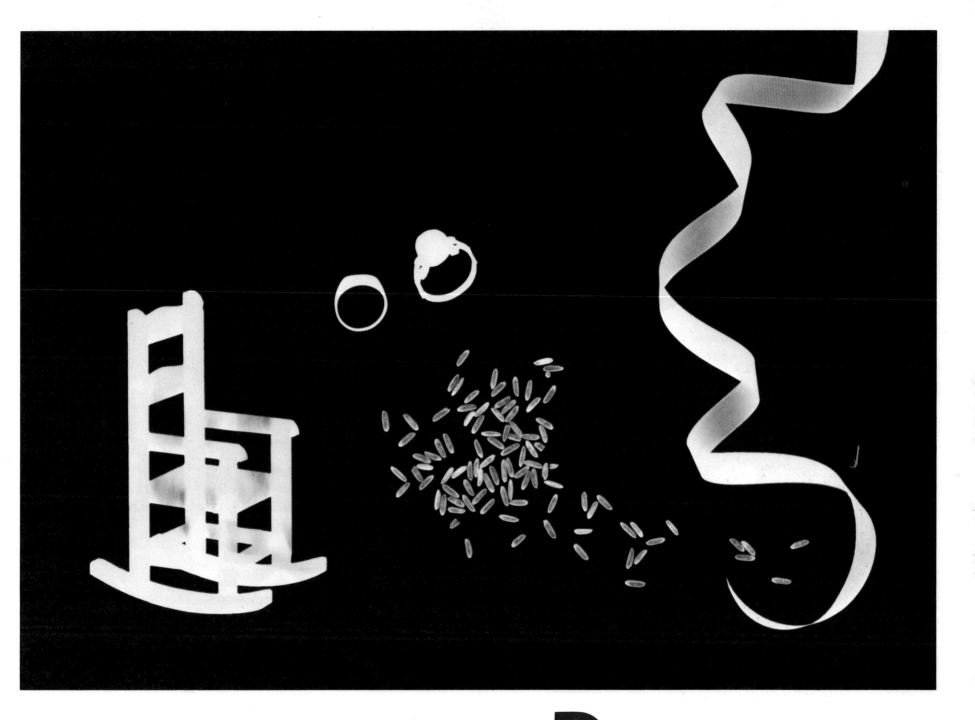

ABCDEFGHIJKLMNOPQ**R**STUVWXYZ

ABCDEFGHIJKLMNOPQR S TUVWXYZ

ABCDEFGHIJKLMNOPQRSTUVWXYZ

ABCDEFGHIJKLMNOPQRST**U**VWXYZ

ABCDEFGHIJKLMNOPQRSTU **V** WXYZ

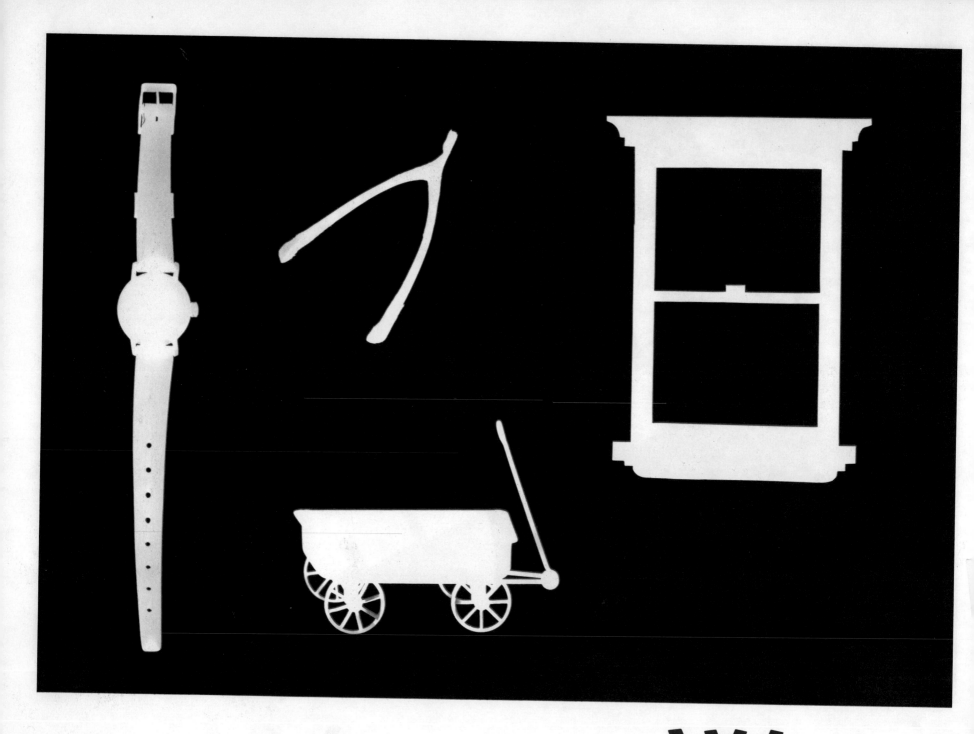

ABCDEFGHIJKLMNOPQRSTUV**W**xyz

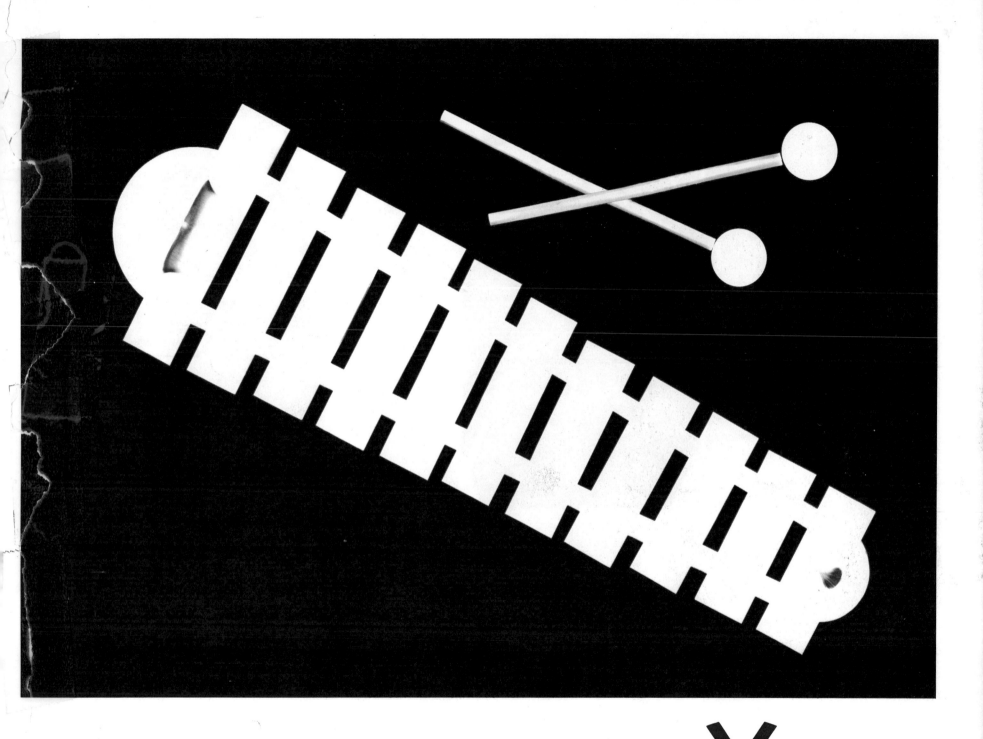

ABCDEFGHIJKLMNOPQRSTUVW**X**yz

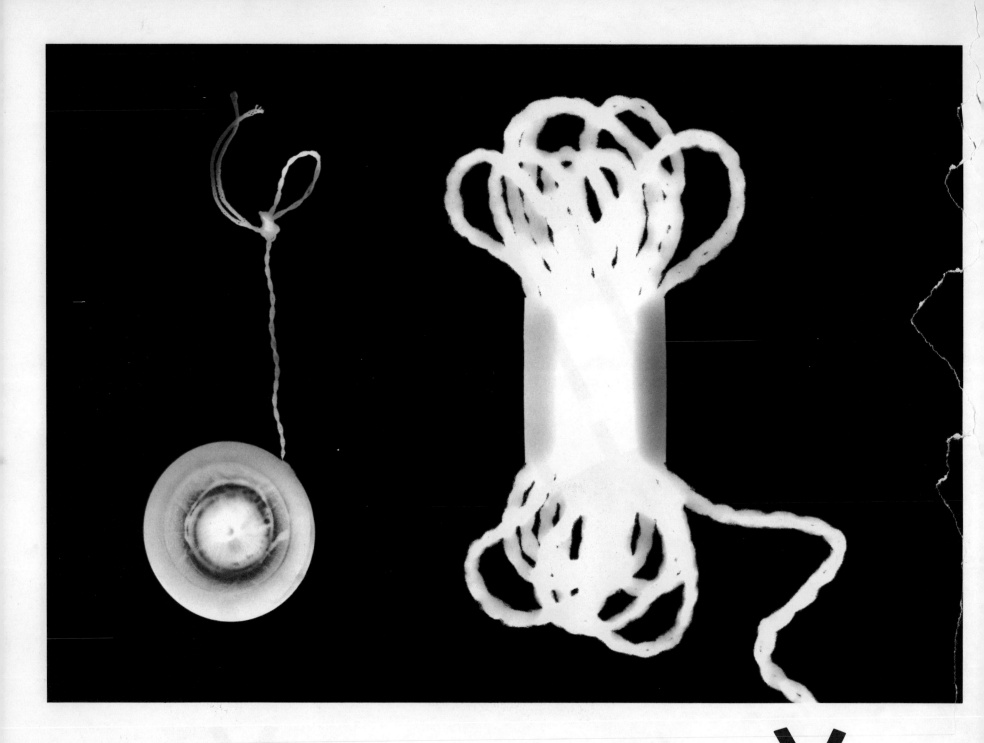

ABCDEFGHIJKLMNOPQRSTUVWXYZ

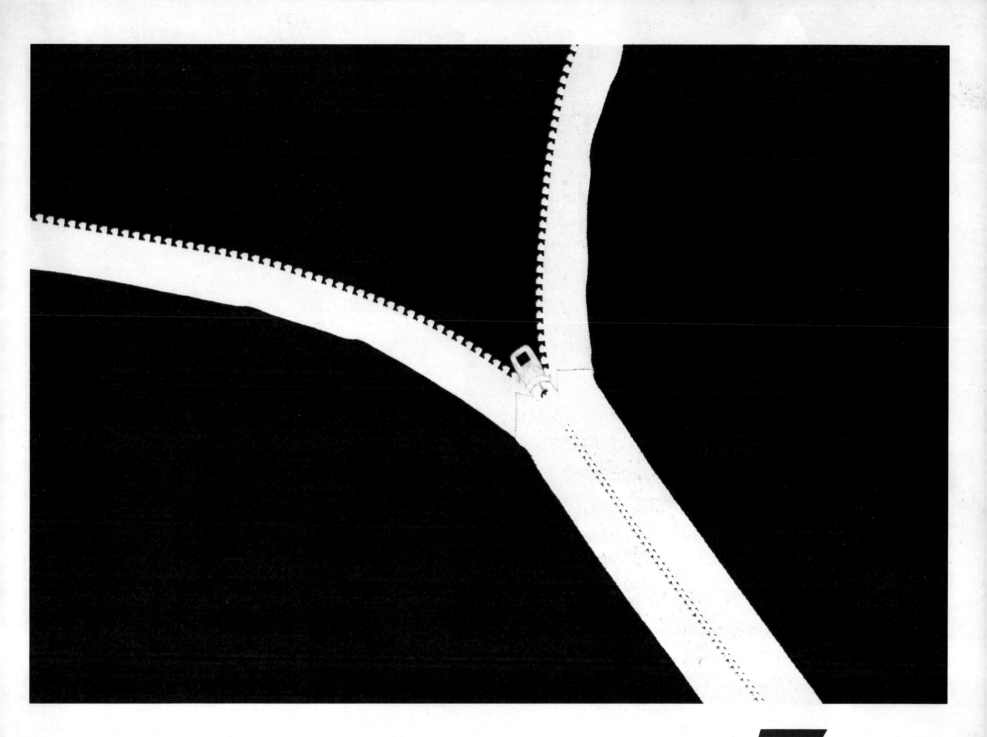

ABCDEFGHIJKLMNOPQRSTUVWXY**Z**

TANA HOBAN's photographs
have been exhibited at the
Museum of Modern Art. She has
won many gold medals and prizes
for her work as a photographer and
filmmaker. And, of course, her
books for children are known and
loved throughout the world.